Turning Over Tables

Learning to Question the "Why" and Advocating for Change

Rev. Jacqueline L. Coleman, MDiv, MA

Fully Restored

Published by Fully Restored
Melrose, Florida

Other Books by This Author

The Yellow Cottage

Woman, Thou Art Restored: Restored to Life to Serve Christ

Biblical Mentoring: What Some of Our Favorite Biblical Characters Teach Us About Mentoring

The Lord has told you what is good,
and this is what he requires of you:
to do what is right, to love mercy,
and to walk humbly with your God.

- Micah 6:8, NIV

Contents

Introduction

I love Thanksgiving! It's that glorious time of year when we gorge ourselves, watch parades, gorge ourselves, watch football, gorge ourselves again, and then sleep! I can't say that I have ever been much into watching the football games, but I know many people who are. Every year, getting together to watch football games is a part of their traditions.

Thanksgiving is a time that overflows with traditions. Maybe that is one of the reasons I like it so much. I can be pretty nostalgic. No two families, even those who are related, celebrate Thanksgiving in the same exact manner. Think for a minute back to when you were a child and what your favorite traditions were. Picture them as they were when you were growing up. Now picture them as they are today. How have those traditions grown and altered over the years? Are there some traditions that have fallen off and you wish you had kept them? Are there some traditions you wish would just go away but you keep them around for the sake of others?

When I was young, my father, who was a cook by trade and still loves to cook, would make Thanksgiving dinner for us. (He is still in charge of Thanksgiving Dinner.) Providing meals has always been a way for him to care for us and let us know that we are loved. Each member of the family was allowed to select a favorite vegetable and, while my father blessed us by preparing a delicious meal with his love, my mother, sisters, and I would enjoy the

Macy's Thanksgiving Day Parade. Although we never celebrated Santa in our home, we didn't eat dinner until after he arrived!

After my husband and I had children, we continued the tradition of allowing each family member to select a favorite vegetable. As time went by, we also started asking our children what pies they wanted and made sure they each had their favorite one ready to go. I really should say "I" here because my husband certainly thinks I overdo this one and, by the plethora of leftover pies, well, I wouldn't say he is wrong, but now it has been going on for so long that I can't get out of it! You can imagine how with five children, three of whom are married, and four grandchildren, how my pie baking has gotten a little bit out of control.

One of our fun family traditions is a pie that no one else has ever heard of: an apple cherry pie. The very first Thanksgiving after our oldest two children were born, I had been making pies and discovered that I had too many apples and too many cherries, but not enough for two more separate pies, so I combined them, apple pie seasoning and all. Although that may sound like an odd combination, it very quickly became a family favorite, especially for my husband. Try it sometime! You'll like it!

Years ago, my mother attempted to come to the rescue of my overabundant pie baking by suggesting we should have pie for breakfast on Thanksgiving morning as well as for dessert. Another tradition started. (We still have too many pies.)

Perhaps you are among those who love to decorate your table all fancy with dishes reserved only for the holidays. Perhaps you invite a large number of guests to dine with you, or maybe you keep the celebration to a small group. Yours might be one of those families who goes around the room and says what you are thankful for. Do you make holiday crafts? Did you grow up in one of those families that forced you to reenact the first Thanksgiving and now you either look back on that time nostalgically or groan with embarrassment? I attempted to have my homeschooled children do this once or twice when they were growing up, but it never seemed to come out quite right, and we quickly gave up on that idea.

We all have traditions in our lives that just "are." Sometimes those traditions become altered over the years simply because they have morphed slowly over time into something new. Sometimes we stand back and look, noticing that a tradition, which may have worked well in the past, is not effective today, so we actively engage in making it better or getting rid of it altogether.

Beyond our Thanksgiving, or other, traditions in our lives, we all have circumstances in life that we participate in or are privy to without questioning what is going on. Many of those circumstances are not of concern. They are harmless to us and to others. Many can, in fact, be positive. However, many circumstances and situations that we humdrum along in life without sitting back to evaluate are more than just superficially "not good," they are detrimental to us and to others.

To alter a tradition, a custom, a practice, that is going on around us, we must first step back, look at it and ask, “Why? Why is this practice occurring, is it okay, and is it something that we should dispose of or alter to keep part of it?” And therein lies the problem that we most often face. We tend to not notice what is going on around us, or even in us. We just keep pushing through life, often in disobedience to what God has for us, not even realizing this disobedience is occurring because we are only doing what we have always done. We fail to make space in our lives for God to point out the wrong and to arrest our attention so that He can turn over our tables, leading us to question the “Why?” and then to advocate for change.

Learn to Question

In three of the Gospels (Matthew, Mark, and John) we can read about Jesus turning over the tables of the money changers. Let's look at John's account:

> 13 It was nearly time for the Jewish Passover celebration, so Jesus went to Jerusalem. 14 In the Temple area he saw merchants selling cattle, sheep, and doves for sacrifices; he also saw dealers at tables exchanging foreign money. 15 Jesus made a whip from some ropes and chased them all out of the Temple. He **drove out** the sheep and cattle, **scattered** the money changers' coins over the floor, and **turned over their tables**. 16 Then, going over to the people who sold doves, he told them, "Get these things out of here. Stop turning my Father's house into a marketplace!" *John 2:13-16, NLT, emphasis mine*

Now, let's read Matthew's account:

> 12 Jesus entered the Temple and began to **drive out** all the people buying and selling animals for sacrifice. He **knocked over the tables** of the money changers and the chairs of those selling doves. 13 He said to them, "The Scriptures declare, 'My Temple will be called a house of prayer,' but you have turned it into a den of thieves!" *Matthew 21:12-13, NLT, emphasis mine*

Back in the days of the Temple, most people had to travel quite a distance to offer sacrifices. It was difficult enough to make the journey with *humans*, let alone animals and agriculture. The selling of animals for sacrifice provided a welcome service to weary worn travelers who gladly paid to purchase their sacrifices instead of lugging them that long way. It also offered, for those who were not Israelite by birth, but who had chosen to follow YHWH, a way to acquire what they needed for their Temple sacrifices.

In addition to needing to purchase animals and agriculture for sacrifice, it was essential for the money the Israelites gave to the Temple to be in the correct currency. There was a prevailing thought that Roman money, due to having an imprint of the emperor, was not acceptable to God. It was necessary, therefore, to change this money into special currency that was only accepted at the Temple.

Think of this like exchanging currency when going to another country. There is always some sort of fee attached to the currency exchange. If we are wise, we will shop around for the place to exchange that has the lowest fee attached.

I recently came back from taking a team on a mission trip to Cambodia and Indonesia. When it comes to exchanging currency in Cambodia, it's easy. The country loves US Dollars (USD). They love USD so much that we didn't even have to do any currency exchanges. We could use our USD, as long as the bills were in pristine condition, anywhere we went. Often, we would receive Cambodian Riel as change, but it was always at a fair rate with virtually no exchange fee. In the cities, we could use our credit cards. Of course, we needed to make sure ahead of time that we were not being charged international fees.

Indonesia on the other hand? Well, let's just say that I spent months researching the best way for our team to have the correct currency to spend in Indonesia. It was a headache. Indonesia does not accept USD, so we either had to find a place to exchange at a high rate, use credit cards with no international fees which were accepted in the cities but not in the outskirts, or pull money out of our bank accounts in Indonesian Rupiah at the few ATMs that would allow us to do so. Unless we had bank accounts that didn't charge international and/or ATM fees, we would be charged here as well. We were limited in our options, but were well-prepared going in.

Unlike going into Cambodia and Indonesia where we had different avenues of exchanging money to compare, those going to the Temple who needed to exchange currency and purchase animals for sacrifice didn't have anywhere else that they could go to cost-compare their exchange fee. Those who participated in the selling of animals and the exchanging of currency were well-aware of this and would take advantage of those who needed their services, rather than loving their brothers and sisters and making it easier on them. The animal sellers and money exchangers would skim quite a bit extra off the top in addition to using unbalanced weights and measures to make it look like those who were coming in to make purchases or currency exchanges were giving them less than they actually were. It was highway robbery!

Just like when we go to another country and need to exchange money or purchase supplies, the idea of having items to purchase for sacrifice and currency exchange readily available was not, in and of itself, a "bad" thing. This availability, if done correctly and in a loving manner, would make the giving of Temple sacrifices more welcoming to those who traveled a great distance as well as those who were not Jewish by blood ancestry. It would make space for them to be included in YHWH's family, and it would show YHWH's love to them. However, a process that could have been designed and implemented in such a way to welcome people in, and it initially may have been just that, became a way in which to keep people out!

As bad as this was, and everyone was aware it was happening, there was a bigger problem at play. For too long, the people had accepted that this was just the way things were supposed to be. They didn't question it; they accepted life as it was, not even dreaming there was another way, with no one willing to question what was happening.

It's like that for us now, isn't it? We plod along in life without asking why things are the way they are. If we happen to notice something that is wrong, unjust, or inhumane we dare not rock the boat. Sadly, more often than not, we fail to notice the wrong because we are quite content in our own little worlds. However, if we take the time to notice what is wrong or harmful in a situation or practice and get involved, we can participate in making it better.

Keep in mind that not all different is bad. In fact, quite a lot of "different" is good and something from which we can learn. Nonetheless, we should learn to always ask "why" because sometimes in asking "why" we uncover a situation that *does* need to be corrected and then we have the opportunity to be a part of the impetus for positive change.

Years ago, I heard a story that has caused me to pause on many occasions:

A girl was in the kitchen with her mother. The mother was baking a ham. Before the mother put the ham in pan, she chopped off both ends. The girl asked her mother, "Mom, why do you always cut off both ends of the ham before cooking it?"

"I don't know," the mother replied. "That is the way my mother always did it."

The next time the mother was at her mother's house and grandma was preparing to bake a ham, grandma chopped off both ends of the ham before she put it in the pan. The mother asked her mother, "Mom, why do you always cut off both ends of the ham before cooking it?"

"I don't know," the grandmother replied. "That is the way my mother always did it."

So, the next time the grandmother was at *her* mother's house and *great* grandma was preparing to bake a ham, *great* grandma chopped off both ends of the ham before she put it in the pan, and the grandmother asked her mother, "Mom, why do you always cut off both ends of the ham before cooking it?"

"Well," great grandma said, "I never have had a pan big enough to fit the whole ham in."

We can laugh at this story, but how often do we follow traditions or practices without knowing why? Granted, there was nothing inherently wrong in this situation, except perhaps the wasting of perfectly good food which many people I know would consider "sinful." The point is, the girl stepped back to notice, questioned "Why?" and discovered the answer. What she did with that information, I'll never know, but she had, through her questioning, been given the opportunity to learn, to evaluate, and to advocate for change based on her new understanding.

What would you say if I dared you to alter something about your Thanksgiving plans this year; if I were to suggest you change it up or try something new? Or, what about this one: what if you were to give up eating this year? What if we were to all make this a day of fasting and prayer instead of gorging ourselves in the name of thanking God for His blessings?

Just to even *think* about changing a Thanksgiving tradition can make us shake in our boots. For years, I had mentioned that some year I would like to order Chinese food instead of cooking a traditional meal but, when it actually came down to it and my entire family agreed to my off-the-wall idea one year, I was so stuck in our Thanksgiving traditions that *I* was the one waffling and driving them crazy with my indecision as whether or not we were actually going to do it. My family called me out on my waffling and ordered the meal.

The people who came to the Temple saw things how they were and did not even dare to think about changing things. They didn't question what was going on, how it had gotten that way, or if it was even right. People were being taken advantage of, and no one was addressing the issue. Those who were benefitting from this arrangement were happy to leave the situation as it was. Those who were financially set enough for it to not affect them personally just kept plodding along in life. Those who were most affected, who were being robbed and struggling to make ends meet, were backed into a corner in which they could not work to change anything without assistance from those who had more power.

As harmful and toxic as this situation was for the poor, and that was most people, the selling of overpriced animals and the weighted exchange of money was a superficial act which stemmed from a much deeper problem. The Israelites were neglecting YHWH's clear instructions to love and care for others. It was necessary for Jesus to arrest the attention of the Israelites by physically turning over their tables in order to call them back into obedience to His Father because they couldn't seem to listen to the instructions that YHWH had already, repeatedly, given them when it came to worshipping Him. YHWH had already told His people what was important, what He required of them, and that was to love Him by loving others.

Questions for Reflection

1. What are your family traditions, favorite or not, and why do you keep them? This doesn't have to be Thanksgiving related.

2. Have you ever tried to alter any of your family traditions? Was this successful or did it meet with grumbling from others?

3. Have you ever questioned any of your family traditions? Or questioned things going on around you? What did you learn?

4. Do you sit back, learn, and question the "Why?" In what way?

5. Share a time that you were an advocate for positive change in a situation that you noticed was wrong. If you haven't done this, can you think of any situations in which you could get involved as an advocate to help guide people towards more Christ-like behavior?

6. Share a time that you noticed a situation that was wrong but did nothing to help advocate for change? Why? Is there anything that you would do differently today?

Let Your Light Shine

Let's take a look at Isaiah 1:10-17, NLT (emphasis mine):

10 Listen to the Lord, you leaders of "Sodom."
Listen to the law of our God, people of
"Gomorrah."
11 "What makes you think I want all your sacrifices?"
says the Lord.
"**I am sick** of your burnt offerings of rams
and the fat of fattened cattle.
I get no pleasure from the blood
of bulls and lambs and goats.
12 When you come to worship me,
who asked you to parade through my courts with
all your ceremony?
13 **Stop bringing me your meaningless gifts**;
the incense of your offerings disgusts me!
As for your celebrations of the new moon and the
Sabbath
and your special days for fasting—
they are all sinful and false.
I want no more of your pious meetings.
14 **I hate** your new moon celebrations and your annual
festivals.
They are a burden to me. **I cannot stand them**!

15 When you lift up your hands in prayer, **I will not
look.**
Though you offer many prayers, I will not listen,
for your hands are covered with the blood of
innocent victims.

16 Wash yourselves and be clean!
Get your sins out of my sight.
Give up your evil ways.

Wow! That's harsh! And ironic. YHWH had told His people to build a Temple for Him and to bring sacrifices and celebrations. They were to bring very specific sacrifices and very specific celebrations in very specific ways and at very specific times. In fact, He was so serious and detailed about these sacrifices and celebrations that we often find ourselves tripping over all the details involved in them while trying to read the Pentateuch.

But let's go on. Verse 17 says (emphasis mine),

17 Learn to do **good.**
Seek **justice**.
Help the **oppressed**.
Defend the **cause of orphans.**
Fight for the **rights of widows**.

What do these verses that follow directly after God's rejection of sacrifices and celebration tell us? Let's flesh this out a little.

In Isaiah 49, YHWH told Israel that they are to be a light to all the nations. The people of Israel have been set apart to be watched by other nations so that God, showing His power, authority, glory, and love through them would become desired above all other gods and those who are looking on will turn to the God of Israel as their God. In other words, God told His people that they have been put in such a position that they are being watched. Whether the Israelites obey Him or disobey Him, the other nations are watching. Their special nation, hand selected by YHWH (Deuteronomy 7:6), has a very serious responsibility to not only not lead people astray, but to lead other nations to Him.

Whenever I think about Israel as a light to others, I am reminded of the old Sunday School Chorus, "This Little Light of Mine."

> This little light of mine,
> I'm gonna let it shine.
> This little light of mine,
> I'm gonna let it shine.
> This little light of mine,
> I'm gonna let it shine,
> let it shine, let it shine, let it shine.

In order to give credit where credit was due, I looked up this song to find out who the composer was. I ended up uncovering a lot more than I had imagined. As it turns out, this hymn is much older than I had thought. It was first sung as a Black Spiritual, part of the liturgy that developed after enslaved people were forced to adopt a Western form of Christianity. It then morphed and developed in different contexts so much over the years that today, while there are guesses as to its original hymnwriter, no one really knows who exactly that was.[1]

I discovered that the song has many different stanzas that have been added or modified over the years, and that the lyrics I recall most vividly don't even appear in most hymnals. You know, or you might not know, the ones about not letting Satan blow the light out or refusing to hide the light under a bushel. Nonetheless, every stanza I came across still reflects the scriptural text on which the song is based and is part of the beatitudes, instructions for Kingdom living, that are found in Matthew 5.

> [14] "You are the light of the world. A town built on a hill cannot be hidden. [15] Neither do people light a lamp and put it under a bowl. Instead they put it on its stand, and it gives light to everyone in the house. [16] In the same way, let your light shine before others, that they may see your good deeds and glorify your Father in heaven. *Matthew 5:14-16, NIV*

But what does Jesus mean by this? Simply put, as Christians, as Christ-followers, we are visible! What we do, good or bad, is a representation of our walk with Christ and, whether that representation is an accurate or a distorted picture of who Christ is, people are watching. People decide whether or not they want to begin a relationship with Jesus based greatly on our behavior as Believers. Let's face it. Once we declare ourselves to be a Christian, people begin to comb over lives carefully and watch to see if they can find a discrepancy between what we *say* we believe and how we *live* our lives.

Just like the Israelites, we have been and continue to be invited to share God's love with the world. In fact, that is what it means to step into God's call on our lives. First and foremost, we love God, but we love God by loving others and loving others means that we share His love with them using words and actions and those words and actions must match (Matthew 22:36-40)!

Christ-followers are lights. If we put a light under a bowl, what happens? It goes out, or is at least hidden, right? Why would someone light a light just to cover it? They wouldn't! Our lights go on stands and the whole world sees.

Why? So that others can come to know Christ. But if our light is shining falsely, in a way that casts shadows by not living as one who is saved by grace and called into the task of guiding others to that same grace, then we cause people to stumble and head in the wrong direction or turn away entirely.

I live in Florida. Thus, my family has experienced more than one hurricane with a power outage. When power outages occur, we never know how long that outage will last, so we need to be proactive in our preparations. We have a cabinet above the sink that everyone knows about. It is filled with candles, lighters, batteries, and flashlights so that we are prepared when the inevitable does happen.

Just yesterday, when attempting to find a battery to put into a game for the grandchildren, we discovered that some of the batteries were out of date. Hurricane season will be here before we know it, so I was reminded of the necessity to make sure that cabinet is checked and ready to go. Stocking that cabinet doesn't do any good if the supplies in it are not kept up to date. That led me to thinking about how our spiritual lives might be initially stocked well, but if we do not keep them up to date or maintained, our lights won't work properly.

When we light those candles or flashlights that we keep at the ready, we will often only light one area of the house at a time so that we can conserve light for the unknown amount of time that we will need it. Still, in those lit areas, there are shadowy places, places that we can trip over if we don't turn our lights to aim in the direction that we are moving. When we turn that light, it can often mean that the others who were using that light end up more in the shadows momentarily.

God's light is similar in that it lights the area to shine the way for others. It is the opposite in that it shines everywhere at all times, but when we are not living as we should as Christ-followers, we end up casting shadows and helping people trip. It is not God who casts the shadows; as sinful humans saved by grace, we cast them. These shadows are not cast as a result of God's light in us, but rather as a result of our inability to fully live as children of God's light.

We are all guilty of looking at others and not loving them as God has asked us to love. We get comfortable in our own spaces and don't even recognize this has happened. We shut people out of our churches and our homes and our daily living just because they act or think a certain way. This hypocrisy of saying that we love because God loves us and then using our actions to do otherwise casts shadows and turns people away.

I grew up in Christian Camping. At our camp,

every week during the summer we had many different groups of campers in. One of those groups was a weekly Adults with Special Needs Camp. At the time, it was called, "AMR: Adults with Mental Retardation." I am glad to see that it has changed names over the years. ***How dehumanizing was that to call people "retarded?"*** Unfortunately, "retarded" was the prevailing terminology for people with all sorts of mental or physical disabilities until the late 1900's. I am thankful that people noticed something wrong, questioned it, and stepped in to advocate successfully for change.

At this camp in Ocean Park, Maine, my mother served as the camp nurse and my father served as the camp cook. In my elementary years, my parents always made sure that my family sat with the Adults with Special Needs for our meals and participated in their camp activities as much as possible. Why? So that we would learn to see our camp guests as people who were made in God's image, not as outcasts to be looked down on.

Was it "gross" sometimes, especially as an elementary age child, to watch these adults eat or otherwise drool? Was it difficult as we got older and served as their counselors to help them take care of their personal needs? Of course, but my sisters and I learned to see people as who they are, beautifully created in the image of God and worthy of having God's light shone on them so that they could know they were loved and learn to love Him. And you know what? After a time of really getting to know these wonderful people, we were able to look past the "gross" and the difficult to simply serve and love. My sisters and I will forever be grateful for what our parents intentionally instilled in us.

We are to be lights for all, not just those that *we* in our sinful selves deem as worthy, and that light must shine Truth, not hypocrisy. When we march boldly into our places of worship, if we cannot truly say that we are loving others as God intended, then all our prayers and liturgies mean nothing.

Isaiah 56:7, quoted by Jesus in the temple when He turned over the tables of the moneychangers, declares that God's house is to be a house of prayer for ***all people***, not just the Jews, and not just the Jews who can afford to bring sacrifices. And there can be no mistaking what Micah states so clearly in Micah 6:6-8, NLT, (emphasis mine).

6 What can we bring to the Lord?
Should we bring him burnt offerings?
Should we bow before God Most High
with offerings of yearling calves?

7 Should we offer him thousands of rams
and ten thousand rivers of olive oil?
Should we sacrifice our firstborn children
to pay for our sins?

8 No, O people, **the Lord has told you what is good**,
and this is what he **requires** of you:
to **do what is right**, to **love mercy**,
and to **walk humbly with your God**.

Bringing our sacrifices to God demands that we care for others, especially those who cannot care for themselves. We care for others by noticing what is wrong in this world and then seeking change. We cannot notice what is wrong when we are so stuck in ***our*** way of doing things that we cannot see another way.

The Israelites were so stuck in the action of their sacrifices, in following the prescriptions of the sacrifices that they had been given, that they were failing to notice and love those around them. Their sacrifices had become something to accomplish rather than God's original intention of bringing them into His presence and bringing others with them. Their lights were not shining as YHWH had intended for them to shine and, therefore, were not effective in sharing His love to other nations. They needed their tables turned over so that they could reset and refocus.

We must learn to question so that we can listen to God and allow Him to reset our lights so that they shine in a way that reflects Christ *as He is*, not as who we think He should be.

Questions for Reflection

1. Can you think of any acts of sacrifice or celebration in your life that have become simply actions? What are they?

____
____
____
____
____
____
____
____

2. What does it mean to you that as a Christ-follower you are always pointing others to or reflecting others away from Jesus?

____
____
____
____
____
____
____
____

3. What are you bringing to God that you, perhaps, need to take a step back and re-evaluate?

____
____
____

4. Where or who is God calling you to love more? Where is He calling you too be more of a light that points truthfully and accurately to Him? What action steps can you take?

Be Obedient

And so, dear brothers and sisters, I plead with you to give your bodies to God because of all he has done for you. Let them be a ***living*** *and holy sacrifice—the kind he will find* ***acceptable****.*

Romans 12:1, NLT, emphasis mine

A sacrifice given to God is always the best we have to offer. To give God the best, we must give Him want He wants; we must do as He asks and what He asks is for us to share His love with others. Sharing His love is messy because people are messy. Sharing His love stretches us and asks us to try new things because different isn't always bad. When different is bad it's because people don't know Christ and they won't know Christ unless we get involved in their lives and become Christ embodied for them.

It's important to remember this: *God's math is not the same as our math.* A sacrifice is not having something negatively removed from us; a sacrifice is our best given to God so that He can multiply it. Sacrifices grow even when, and especially when, we feel stretched out of what we know because it is in that stretching that God is building us increasingly into Jesus.

A living sacrifice continues to grow as it continues to sacrifice in doing God's will, which is to love others by showing His love so that they, too, can know Him. A living sacrifice cannot be presented to

God as worship unless it is living and if it is not growing it is not living. Once it stops growing, it becomes a dead animal presented to God as an action without meaning. An action without meaning is self-serving. When we serve only ourselves, we may do things that make ourselves feel good, but we will fail to connect with God, thus we will fail to be obedient in sharing His love as lights in this world.

In Isaiah 1, God said, “Stop bringing me your meaningless acts. Bring me your living actions of loving others and enjoy my presence!”

But, just as in His reprimand to the Israelites and I dare say us in Isaiah, sometimes God has to turn over our tables in order to get us to listen and obey! Sometimes He has to shake things up to get us to change things, in order to get us to reset and refocus. When Jesus came in to address the marketplace that had been set up in the Temple, He wasn’t simply saying, “Stop selling things in my Father’s House,” He was saying, “You aren’t listening to what I told you! Pay attention to what My Father is saying!”

What is God saying, though? Despite the fact that the Israelites were not listening, God had been very clear about what He was asking from them, and He is asking the same from us. He has spoken, and we refuse to listen. He jumps in to turn over our tables only ***after*** He has already spoken, sometimes multiple times and in multiple ways.

Think about how many times YHWH spoke to the Israelites, clearly telling them what He required of them and then, after they would not obey, sending them into exile, or sending other painful circumstances their way in order to turn over their tables and get them to reset into obedience. Jesus turning over the tables in the Temple was another example of how God kept trying to get His people to turn back to Him. God is clear about how we are to join Him in His mission and we, in our stubbornness and selfishness, cannot hear.

Several years ago, God called me to leave a church that I loved. I loved leading the music and the choirs. This was a time that was formative in developing my Theology of Worship. It was a joy to learn through a girls' ministry that I had, with the help of others, launched 15 years prior. I loved the people at this church and the way that they cared for one another. Through these ministries, God grew my gifts of pastoring/shepherding, teaching, administration, faith, leadership, giving, encouragement, and knowledge, among others. I met Christian brothers and sisters who became family. I do not regret a moment of this time.

Unfortunately, this church and the people in this church were participatory in stifling God's call on my life. God had called me into serving Him as a pastor and this church did not agree with women serving in ministry leadership. I loved these people and I did not wish to leave them but, as with any disobedience we have to God's call on our lives, when we do not obey, we cannot grow. And that's where I was. Not only had my spiritual growth not increased but it had also leveled off and had gotten stuck. When we live that way long enough, we end up going backwards in our spiritual growth and our lights shine with shadows that turn others away.

God had told me it was time to leave but I wasn't listening to God's *words*, so He stepped in and turned over my table. It was painful. I went through many hurtful circumstances with friends and with family. These are circumstances from which I am still healing today.

My husband had told me years before I accepted it was time to leave that he was ready to go. Through this and through other more gentle ways, God had spoken and I had not listened. While I do not regret a moment of my time at that church and God used it to grow me in many ways during it as well as every time I reflect back on that experience, I cannot help but wonder if I had listened to God's gentle nudging earlier if I would not have had to have my table turned over so abruptly so that I could once again dwell in His presence in obedience.

God rescued His people from Egypt and He established His tabernacle with them so that He could be in their presence and they could be in His (Exodus 25:8). To "tabernacle" is to dwell. God wanted His people to be with Him. He wanted His people to Sabbath, to rest and be in His presence.

But even before the physical tabernacle was established, God dwelt among His people leading and guiding them. Exodus 13:21-22 tells us,

> 21 By day the Lord went ahead of them in a pillar of cloud to guide them on their way and by night in a pillar of fire to give them light,

so that they could travel by day or
night. [22] Neither the pillar of cloud by day nor
the pillar of fire by night left its place in front
of the people. NIV

Have you ever wondered why most people love campfires so much? Have you ever stopped to consider how so many people love to gaze up at the clouds? There is something cozy about the togetherness of sitting around a campfire or lying on your back with others pointing out shapes in the clouds. God lived among His people in a cloud by day and a pillar of fire by night. Perhaps there is something about the awesomeness of fire and the beauty of clouds that makes us feel closer to God.

Through the presence of both the fire by night and the cloud by day, God had provided a way for His people to be with Him, to be in His presence all the time. He intentionally dwelt among them so that they could be with Him and, by establishing the tabernacle and the required sacrifices, He invited them into an even closer relationship.

The problem came when His people got so caught up in following the letter of the law that they lost sight of the bigger picture.

It's like that saying, "You can't see a forest through the trees." The Israelites were so hung up on making sure to cross every "t" and dot every "i" that they lost sight of God's command to join Him in loving others. They even made laws around the laws so that people couldn't get close to the initial law to break it. They neglected caring for those in need so that when they brought their sacrifices to God, which were not wrong in themselves, they were doing so in disobedience to God's primary command to them to love others. When we live in disobedience to what God asks of us, we hinder ourselves in growing spiritually.

The good news is that we have a God who wants us to come to Him and repent. He isn't going anywhere and He is waiting with open arms for us to step back into being obedient. We can listen to His gentle nudging and need not wait for a painful turning over of our tables.

Lest we think that we needn't think about where our hearts are at today when we come into God's presence, let's remember what Jesus told us in Matthew 5:23-24,

> **23** "Therefore, if you are offering your gift at
> the altar and there remember that your brother
> or sister has something against you, **24** leave
> your gift there in front of the altar. First go and be reconciled to them; then come and offer your gift. *NIV*

God wanted His children, just as He had commanded in Genesis, to care for His Creation which meant caring for people (Genesis 1:26-28). Yes, He had very prescribed methods of sacrifice, but the Israelites lost the message of being in His presence and caring for His Creation in the action of completing those sacrifices. They failed to connect with Him. They were more focused on offering sacrifices than they were on caring for God by caring for His people and simply enjoying being in His presence. They failed to understand that God's desire was for them to care for people, to love them with His love, and to get to know Him far more than it was for them to formally bring Him burnt offerings (Hosea 6:6)

This is no less true today. In fact, it is even more so. Unlike the Israelites of long ago who had to physically go to the tabernacle or the temple,

> we are the temple of the living God. As God has said,
> "I will live with them
> and walk among them,
> and I will be their God,
> and they will be my people."
> *2 Corinthians 6:16b, NIV*

God is within us. We worship Him individually as well as corporately. We worship Him privately and we worship Him among other believers. We should be worshipping Him all the time and in all we do. Both individual and corporate worship are necessary to our spiritual growth and both require obedience to what He is calling us to do, to join His mission by loving others to Him in whatever way it is that He has called us to do that, otherwise our sacrifices are empty loud gongs and annoying clanging cymbals that hang over people's heads creating confusion as to what Truth actually is (1 Corinthians 13:1) and placing us in a position where God is saying, "Stop! If you say you love Me, join My mission and love others, or your empty worship, your empty sacrifices, mean nothing!"

Being a “living and holy sacrifice – the kind [God] will find acceptable” requires obedience (Romans 12:1, NLT). Obedience requires that we love others. We cannot love others without noticing what is going on around us and questioning the “why,” testing circumstances to see if they are in line with being lights that shine accurate reflections of Christ and advocating for change if they do not. When we live as holy sacrifices, we are obedient in loving others so that our worship can be as God intended, in line with what He asks of us, to join in His mission and be in His presence.

Questions for Reflection

1. In what area of your life is God calling you to stretch and grow?

2. How do you feel about the fact that God wants to dwell with us and that He wants us to dwell with Him?

3. Do you have a brother or sister with whom you need to be reconciled? What steps are you going to take to make this reconciliation happen?

4. What does it mean to you that you that without loving others as God has called us to, that your remote action sacrifices of worship are worthless?

5. Where is God calling you to be more obedient? What are you going to do about it?

Stop Fighting

*10 "**Be still**, and know that I am God!*
I will be honored by every nation.
I will be honored throughout the world."
11 The Lord of Heaven's Armies is here among us;
the God of Israel is our fortress.

Psalm 46:10-11, NLT, emphasis mine

Let's take a step back here, lest we are tempted to think that we can actually love others on our own. God has invited us to love others through His love. God has invited us to be in His presence through His love.

The people who hurt me at the church I left? I have forgiven them and I see them as hurting themselves, but I haven't forgiven them because I in myself have some supernatural power for forgiving people. I have forgiven them because God has given me the gift of being able to forgive. I can forgive through His love and through His power and through His ability to see all people as broken and needing Him. If I were not able to forgive them through Him, I could not in good conscience come into God's presence to worship Him, but I could not forgive them without Him.

Do you see the balance in this? I can be in God's presence because He has invited me to be in His presence. However, I cannot be wholly in His presence without leaning into God to love others. If I come into His presence without loving as He has asked me to do and enabled me to do, then I sit before Him with empty sacrifices. But, and this is important, I cannot do it on my own; I must allow ***Him*** to do it! All the balance rests in Him. My only task is to be obedient, *and* I must lean on Him in order to be obedient because I cannot do it in my own power.

At age 7, in second grade, I had no idea at the time that I was part of the "in-crowd." That is, until that "fateful" day, anyway…the one in which I befriended a lonely girl on the playground and my best friend at the time said I could no longer be friends with "*them*" (plural) if I was going to be friends with "*her*." And, yes, I still remember "*her*" name. Actually, I still remember *both* of their names.

When that statement was made to me that proved to seal my separation as an "outcast" for the remainder of my school career, I felt a sudden rush of something come over me and kind of "take over." I thought my friend was speaking utter nonsense and I did not refrain from telling her as much.

I learned as an adult that that sudden rush coming over me is what many would call, and I would agree, the Crisis Point of Sanctification or the moment that I released all control to the Holy Spirit. While I had chosen to follow Christ at the age of 5, something must have been happening in my life at the age of 7 that caused God to turn over my table to make sure that my spiritual growth was pointing straight toward Him, was resting in Him, so that I could continue to grow and be stretched in Him.

I spent my school career in academics with the "in-crowd" because that was the "smart" crowd, taunted and teased all the while, but God used that separation that had occurred when I was only 7 to protect me from any sort of temptation that may have been drawn to come my way over the years, saving me from interactions with alcohol, drugs, sex, bad behavior, etc. He had turned over my table in order to protect me and to give me space to grow in Him and Him alone, cementing my identity as a Child of the Living God rather than leaving me to struggle with the inevitable question most teenagers have of, "Who am I?"

Sure, there were some painful times, like when I tried to throw a Valentine's Day Party to gain my "friends" back and no one showed up. But, at the same time, just before high school graduation, God gave something back to me.

During those many years, the Holy Spirit gave me the strength and the ability and the fortitude to stand strong. That same girl who had ousted me in second grade had been watching my witness as we grew up together and wrote in my yearbook that she wished she had had the strength to stand by her convictions all those years like she had seen that I had. Granted, I didn't follow Christ so obediently to be lauded by others, but it was like God was giving me a little stamp of approval for learning to listen rather than fight Him.

Somewhere along the way, in those early elementary years, God gave me my life verse. There are times that I have had other verses jump out to me as important, and I know that for many their "life" verses can change as the years go by, so I have tried to be open to mine changing but everything in my life, especially God, points to this life verse never changing:

Ephesians 6:12: For we wrestle not against flesh and blood, but against principalities, against powers, against the rulers of the darkness of this world, against spiritual wickedness in high places.

King James, of course…I am a child of the 80's and still love King James!

God turned over my table when I was 7 in a way that was painful to me at the time in order to give me something better, in order to give me what was right. He took that space in my life to prepare me for what was ahead. He gave me a broken heart for what breaks His. He taught me to love ALL people.

When God gave me the life verse of Ephesians 6:12, He gave me the ability to see that I was not fighting the *people* who were being ugly because they themselves were also broken and needing to meet Him. I did not retaliate ugly with ugly, and I stood firm in loving everyone who crossed my path because they were themselves being deceived and needed the love of Jesus in their lives. God instilled in me a lifestyle witness which has proven to be effective in showing Jesus to others. *He* did the work in me, and *He* continues to do the work in me, that makes my words match my actions.

God invited me into His presence, and He

invited me to love people with His love, but I could not get there in my own power. We do not need to battle to be in God's presence. He has invited us in, and we can lean on Him to give us the strength to stay there.

"Be still," God says! "Stop wrestling. Sit in my presence."

Psalm 46:10 is often translated as "Be still and know that I am God." Just as often, it is translated, "Cease striving and know that I am God." And better yet, "Stop fighting and know that I am God."

Stop fighting God. Know that He is God, the Creator who holds everything, including our best interests and our well-being in His hands, and allow Him to take control. Sit with Him. Listen to what He has to say. Relax in His arms and He will lift you higher than you could ever imagine.

The beauty of that higher is that He has invited us, through the power of His Spirit living in us, to be His witness, to be a light, to those who are living in darkness, to those who are striving to do it on their own.

God will be "be honored by every nation [and] throughout the world" (Psalm 46:10b, NLT). For now, He has invited us to join Him, He has asked us to sit with Him, to let Him love us so that we can love others with His love in order that those others learn to sit in His presence as well. He does not need us in order to accomplish His mission, rather He invites us in to be a part of what He is already doing. When we learn to stop fighting Him and to allow Him to work through us, we are blessed to join in a work that is beyond anything that we could begin to imagine or conceive.

Questions for Reflection

1. Are you depending on God for the ability to love others, or are you trying to love others in your own strength? Can you share some examples?

   ____
   ____
   ____
   ____
   ____
   ____
   ____
   ____

2. How are you when it comes to forgiving others? Do you try to forgive in your strength, or do you allow forgiveness to flow from you out of God's strength?

   ____
   ____
   ____
   ____
   ____
   ____
   ____
   ____

3. In what ways are you wrestling God?

   ____
   ____
   ____

4. Are you able to see people who hurt you as broken and needing the love of Jesus? How do you invite them in? What spaces do you hold open for them to experience God's love?

5. How comfortable are you just being in God's presence? Do you simply embrace it, or do you find yourself struggling to get there? In what way?

Dwell in His Presence

[14] The Word became flesh and made his ***dwelling*** *among* ***us.*** *We have* ***seen*** *his glory, the glory of the one and only Son, who came from the Father, full of grace and truth.*

John 1:14, NIV, emphasis mine

Did you catch that word "dwelling?" Jesus came and dwelt among us. He tabernacled among us. He made His home with us. The glory that could be seen by the Hebrews in a cloud by day and a pillar of fire by night (Isaiah 40:38) had over time been relegated to an idea that God could only be found in the Temple, and that only by following prescribed sacrifices down to the letter. Now, when God in the form of Jesus had become tangible and visible to all even standing in the Temple among them, the people were so stuck in their traditions that they could not see Him! They were so focused on their *doing* that they neglected their *being.* They neglected the invitation that God had given them to sit with Him, to dwell with Him.

Doing is one of my specialties. I like lists. I like lists so much that if I do something that was not on my list, I will add it to my list so that I can check it off as complete. I am guilty of getting caught up in the check lists of administration in a church instead of remembering to be with people. In fact, I am guilty of being frustrated with having to be with people when I have check lists to complete.

This is not because I do not want to be with people, I just have a tendency to put my list ahead of God's list. God's list tells me that people are more important, but I get so caught up in the *doing* that often and sadly, and to the detriment of loving people as God loves them, I add people to my "list" rather than simply allowing *being* to happen.

I am guilty of doing that with God as well. I tend to focus so much on what needs to get accomplished on my list that I either fail to spend time *being* with God or get frustrated when my doing gets interrupted by His *being*, by *His* plans for my day.

Jesus, on the last day of the Feast of Tabernacles, said,

> [38] "Whoever believes in me, as Scripture has said, rivers of living water will flow from within them." [39] By this he meant the Spirit, whom those who believed in him were later to receive. *John 7:38, NIV*

Now, read it in the Amplified Version.

> [38] "He who believes in Me [who adheres to, trusts in, and relies on Me], as the Scripture has said, 'From his innermost being will flow *continually* rivers of living water." *John 7:38*

Our bodies are temples of the Holy Spirit (1 Corinthians 6:19) and it is through the indwelling of the Holy Spirit that we are given the power to be witnesses of Christ and what He has done, is still doing, in us (Acts 1:8).

The Holy Spirit teaches us (John 14:26). The Holy Spirit enables us to love others and to keep God's commands (John 14:15-17). When we are filled with the Holy Spirit, we are holy ground because anywhere that God is, is holy. It is set apart. We are set apart. We are holy because God is holy and dwells within us (1 Peter 1:16). Therefore, we are holy representatives of God and His love anywhere we go.

We cannot afford to think that this holiness is only active when we are in our brick-and-mortar places of worship, rather this holiness goes with us wherever we are and it is this holiness that must be the light that others see. Through the indwelling of the Holy Spirit, "rivers of living water…flow *continually*" out of us and onto others (John 7:38, AMP).

David is often referred to as a "Man after God's own Heart." We know he made plenty of mistakes, terrible mistakes; mistakes that find us asking, "How could David have done this and still have become King?" These mistakes serve to make him relatable to us, but how in the world could David have earned this title? Perhaps it's because he kept trying. Perhaps it's because when his light was casting shadows and God turned his table over, and over, and over, he repented and went back to following God more closely. Perhaps it's because he understood that God is present everywhere, not just behind four walls; that God truly does dwell with us and wants us to dwell with Him. We are blessed with the richness of the multitude of psalms David wrote that portray his depth of understanding on this matter. David got it! (Psalm 63)

God wanted the presence of His people, all the time, not just in the Temple. This has been the same since creation. In fact, this is so true that God sent His Son to be a visible representation of what God had never stopped telling His people.

> 16 For God so loved the world that he gave his
> one and only Son, that whoever believes in
> him shall not perish but have eternal
> life. 17 For God did not send his Son into the
> world to condemn the world, but to save the
> world through him. 18 Whoever believes in
> him is not condemned, but whoever does not
> believe stands condemned already because
> they have not believed in the name of God's
> one and only Son. 19 This is the verdict:
> Light has come into the world, but people
> loved darkness instead of light because their
> deeds were evil. 20 Everyone who does evil
> hates the light, and will not come into the light
> for fear that their deeds will be exposed. 21 But
> whoever lives by the truth comes into the
> light, so that it may be seen plainly that what
> they have done has been done in the sight of
> God. *John 3:16-21, NIV*

Jesus spoke all around the Israelite communities with a visible Word and the people could not hear Him. They were so caught up in their actions that they could not hear the message. They couldn't see God living with them so, Jesus turned over their tables. He said, "Stop this! Pay attention! I Am here! Sit at my feet! Love others and tell them about Me!"

Do you ever feel as if God is turning over your table? Do you let Him? Or do you wrestle with Him?

Mondays in a church office are often filled with Pastors and staff trying to get checklists accomplished of items that have been leftover from the week before as well as items that will help them move more smoothly into everything that is coming up. Mondays are also filled with people from the church, or not from the church, dropping by, emailing, or calling with their items that are leftover or need to get accomplished or concerns that they have. People swing by just to talk and catch up, in need of prayer, or with burdens that they want to discuss with a listening and caring ear.

It is for this reason that on Mondays, especially, God has taught me to, instilled in me the necessity of, setting my own checklist aside. I have learned to love Mondays when I can get to know people in a more informal setting, help meet their needs, or simply listen to what they have to say. I have learned to embrace Mondays as a fun yet often heartbreaking and grueling day in which the first item on my checklist has become, "God, how are you going to interrupt my checklist today? What is your agenda? Give me an open heart to love and embrace all who will come my way today."

When I set aside my checklist, sit at God's feet, and embrace what He has in store for my day, I end my day, no matter how hard it was, with a peace and a joy that can come from no other place than obediently dwelling with Him.

God is always trying to interrupt our plans for something better, but how often do we get angry or frustrated with Him for doing so? How often do we simply ignore Him altogether? When we do this, not only do we fail to dwell well in His presence, but we miss out on personal spiritual growth as well as opportunities to love others with His love.

When my children were young, my mother told me to pick one daily task to accomplish and to not get upset or frustrated when even that didn't happen. My children were/are more important than any task and spending time with them was/is crucial.

Admittedly, that was much easier when my children were small and had so many needs that they could not do without me. Sadly, I often fail in this now. Granted, they don't need me in the same way, but I am often so busy getting my checklist accomplished that I fail to do well in stopping and spending time with my family. It is often easier to let non-family members interrupt our day than it is family. I strive to be intentional in this area, but I am afraid that I still fail more often than I succeed. This is to my detriment as well as theirs.

God chose to live with us. He calls us to be with Him, to come and sit at His feet at all times and in all places. In doing this He is not calling us to neglect His people. (Matthew 22:35-40) In fact, He is doing just the opposite. Sitting in His presence means that we love others and invite them in to sit in His presence as well.

We cannot *do* the work that God has called us to unless we first learn to *be* with Him. If we don't learn to *be* with Him, we won't even know what that work is, but when we learn to *be* with Him, that work flows from Him and through us into His world.

Questions for Reflection

1. Do you truly see God when He tries to break into your day? How do you react?

2. How comfortable are you with your *doing* flowing out of your *being*? Do you need to be comfortable with this in order to begin allowing it to happen in your life?

3. How can you focus more on setting your plans aside so that you can allow yourself to ebb and flow with God's plans for your day?

4. Who are you neglecting and what intentional steps can you take to remedy this?

Allow God to Turn Over Your Table

[35] One of the Pharisees, an expert in religious law, tried to trap Jesus with this question: [36] "Teacher, which is the most important commandment in the law of Moses?"

*[37] Jesus replied, "'You must love the Lord your God with all your **heart**, all your **soul**, and all your **mind**.' [38] This is the first and greatest commandment. [39] A second is **equally important**: 'Love **your neighbor** as yourself.' [40] The entire law and all the demands of the prophets are based on these two commandments."*

Matthew 22:35-40, NLT emphasis mine

Did you read those words, "equally important?" We know these verses. We quote these verses. But do we *live* these verses?

Do we come into God's house offering sacrifices on Sunday mornings because it is what we are supposed to do or do we sit in His presence all the time knowing that we are doing all we can to bring others into His presence even when it means stepping outside of our secure worlds and trying something new? Do we step into the shoes of others and allow them to teach us? Do we honestly listen to their stories and hear what they have to say, not what we *think* they have to say?

This is one of the reasons that I love taking people on short-term mission trips. Mission trips give people a chance to get out of their hum-drum everyday existence. Mission trips give people a chance to dwell with God in a new and different arena while learning to listen to and learn from other people and other cultures. Mission trips help us to sit back while being stretched and ask God how He wants to grow us. Mission trips give us an opportunity to shake things up while asking God, "What's next?"

Imago Dei means that all people everywhere are made in the image of God.

Missio Dei is the mission of God. As Christ-followers, we are to join in God's mission – not our mission.

Coram Deo is translated to "in the presence of God."

As Christ-followers, as living, breathing temples of God saved by the self-sacrificial act of Jesus' death and resurrection and from whom the Holy Spirit flows like living water on those around us, we are always in the presence of God. The question is, "Are we seeing all people everywhere as made in the image of God and participating fully in the mission of God to love others to Him?

"Do we live, do we dwell continually, in the presence of God or do we try to relegate His presence to Sunday mornings?

And if we are dwelling in the presence of God, are we allowing ourselves to cease striving, to simply *be* so that we can *do* in order that our sacrifices are pleasing and acceptable to God through His power and His power alone?"

I am ordained in the Christian & Missionary Alliance (C&MA). In the C&MA, we refer to ourselves as an Acts 1:8 Family.

> But you will receive power when the Holy Spirit comes upon you. And you will be my witnesses, telling people about me everywhere—in Jerusalem, throughout Judea, in Samaria, and to the ends of the earth." *Acts 1:8, NLT*

Before Jesus ascended to His Father He told His disciples, and us, that we would be His witnesses. We know this. But do we do this with all of ourselves all the time? Even, and especially, in spaces where God has to turn over our tables?

It is interesting to note the order of places that Jesus mentioned in Acts 1:8:

Jerusalem – a city

Judea – a country

Samaria – a city

The ends of the earth – the entire world

Why did Jesus move from a city to a country,

back to a city, and then to the world? When we read this verse, we often read it as if we are moving further and further out and while this is a correct reading, *why* do these instructions come in the order that they do?

Jerusalem is where we are; what is closest to us.

Judea pulls us a little further out of our comfort zones.

Samaria, although we often pass it off as somewhere that is just a little further out than Judea, is far more than that. Witnessing in Samaria is not simply about moving physically further away but about moving out of our comfort zones. The Jews despised the Samaritans so much that they would go out of their way to go around Samaria rather than walking through it, despite the fact that most destinations they were heading towards would be reached faster by going through it. *We must allow our tables to be turned over to reach those whom we are overlooking or, as much as we hate to admit it to ourselves, view as unworthy.*

The Samaritans were Israelites who worshipped God a little differently than the Jews. The Jews looked down on them and considered them unworthy and incapable of being children of God. When Jesus stopped to speak to the Samaritan woman at the well and commissioned her to share His message, He turned over the tables of His disciples by demonstrating the worth of the Samaritans in His eyes and their call to participate in His mission to love others (John 4). When Jesus told the parable of the Good Samaritan, He turned over the tables of His listeners by letting them know that Samaritans could love others, that they were capable and that they themselves were loved (Luke 10:25-37).

Scripture is riddled with accounts of Jesus turning over tables, of Jesus breaking the patterns of tradition to extend His Love to those whom others deemed unworthy and incapable of receiving or giving love.

Think for a minute about such accounts as Jesus healing the woman who was bleeding (Matthew 9:20-22), inviting Zaccheus to dine with Him (Luke 19:1-10), saving the life of the woman who was caught in adultery (John 8:1-11), healing a man's withered hand on the Sabbath (Mark 3:1-6), treating women as equals (Luke 8:1-3), challenging the authority of religious leaders (Matthew 23), and even eating with unwashed hands (Matthew 15:17-18).

I challenge you to pull out your Bibles and find some of those accounts. It won't be difficult. A quick reading of any Gospel will have them jumping right off the pages. You won't have to go far to trip over them.

Then, look at your "normal." Look at the edges of your comfort zones. Is God trying to expand them? Is God saying, "Pay attention! You are tripping over people who need to know I love them!" Until we get to know people, we won't love them as God loves them, but when we get to know them through His love, we will give our lives for them.

Not long after I had started a job as the Missions Pastor at a new church, that church held their annual Car Show Outreach/Summer Camp Fundraiser. One of the reasons people in our church love this event is because it always serves as a great time to build friendships with those whom we already know and begin new friendships with others. At one point in the afternoon, I looked over to where the kids were. They were having a grand time sliding down a giant blow up slide. I thought, "What a great way to connect with the kids. I am going to join them." So, I did.

Those kids had a blast teaching me several different ways to slide down this tube filled with air, and I had an amazing time stepping out of the traditional role of an adult to join in their fun for a few minutes. Was it a little awkward to walk up to children's leaders whom I barely knew and ask if I could go on the slide? Sure, it was! But it was right and it was worth feeling a little out of my element. It was different and it was not bad! These children are now teenagers who continue to feel comfortable around me and I can't help but think that doing things like sliding down a slide with them helped to instill this connection.

Allowing God to turn over our tables opens opportunities to build connections that we would otherwise miss. More importantly, *allowing God to turn over our tables opens doors to share the Gospel with those who might otherwise never hear.*

We don't come to church on Sunday mornings to learn to dwell with God in a "safe" environment.

We come to church on Sunday mornings to learn to dwell with God in *every* environment. Think of church like a huddle. If we stay in the huddle, we can't play the game!

There are things that we do that are perfectly good and not sinful but if they are not intentionally showing love to other people then should we still be doing them?

To be blatantly honest, if something we are doing is not showing God's love then is it, perhaps, actually sinful? Since we have been given the greatest laws, love God and love others (Matthew 22:35-40), and we are to follow them by showing God's love, if we are not sharing God's love, is that not sinful?

We must learn to ask *"why?"* We must understand that what we may unquestioningly accept as "normal" may be considered normal in this world, but it may not be how God desires for us to care for others. We must weigh our traditions and how things are done in this world by God's standards. If they don't measure up, we must advocate for change.

When we tolerate sin, often because we are stuck in our own traditions, our own way of doing things, and do not recognize it as such, we have a major problem. This is more than a superficial surface issue. It is a heart issue, and we need to learn to live in God's presence caring for and loving His people if this is ever going to change. We cannot live as we should without full submission to God which means living, dwelling, in His presence all the time, ready to embrace "interruptions" so that He can lead us to question the "why" and advocate towards change. God is inviting us to help turn over tables.

In Isaiah 1, God called His people to attention for failing to remember to care for ***all people***, especially those who could not care for themselves.

In Isaiah 49, He reminded Israel that they were to be a light for ***all people***.

In Isaiah 56, He clearly stated that His house, His place that He chose to dwell among His people was for ***all people***.

In Micah 6, God reminded the Israelites of His requirement to do justice and to love mercy and to walk with Him.

In Psalm 46, God called us to cease striving and be still with Him.

In John 1, Jesus came to physically make His home with His creation, but the people were so stuck in their traditions, in their actions which had lost meaning, that they did not recognize Him; they failed to see and to understand His presence among them. They were failing to do as God had commanded. So, Jesus turned over their tables to put their attention back on Him. He turns over our tables to do the same, and He invites us to be a part of turning over tables for others.

Pay attention! He is here! Sit at His feet! Love others and tell them about Him! Invite them into His presence!

Questions for Reflection

1. Like the Jews who walked around Samaria, what are you walking around instead of through?

____
____
____
____
____
____
____
____

2. What might God be asking you to do that is out of your comfort zone but well within His calling for your life? How will you respond?

____
____
____
____
____
____
____
____

3. In what ways can you intentionally allow God to stretch and grow you?

____
____
____
____

4. Will you obey and continue to bring a living sacrifice to Him, or will you plod along in your own traditions not noticing where His love requires you to work towards affecting change so that you can bring sacrifices that are not empty? How?

5. How is God turning over your table today?

6. Is God asking you to help turn over the table of someone else? How can you join Him in this?

____
____
____
____
____
____
____
____

7. How can you continue to make space in your lives for God to point out the wrong and to arrest your attention so that He can turn over your table, leading you to question the "Why?" and then to advocate for change?

____
____
____
____
____
____
____
____

References

1. The United Methodist Church. (2023, May 9). History of Hymns: "This Little Light of Mine." Discipleship Ministries. https://www.umcdiscipleship.org/articles/history-of-hymns-this-little-light-of-mine

About the Author

Rev. Jacqueline Coleman holds an MDiv in Global Ministry, an MA in Biblical Studies, and a BS in Youth Ministry. She serves as the Missions and Family Ministries Pastor at Palm Coast Bible Church in Palm Coast, Florida. Her mission is to live obediently, stepping out to boldly love others, while firmly rooted in the knowledge that she is in a spiritual battle that seeks to claim souls.

Jacqui is a Maine girl who married her high school sweetheart. Together, they have 5 adult children, 3 children-in-love, and 4 grandchildren who all love to explore the world.

In addition to enjoying exploring new places with her husband and family, Jacqui loves to read, to write and to teach.

Connect with Jacqui at
iamfullyrestored@gmail.com
or on her website: **jacquicoleman.com**

www.ingramcontent.com/pod-product-compliance
Lightning Source LLC
LaVergne TN
LVHW090535110826
845146LV00003B/1118